The Power of a
Smile

The Power of a Smile

Suzanne S. Bauman

Illustrated by: Corbin Hillam

XULON PRESS

Xulon Press
2301 Lucien Way #415
Maitland, FL 32751
407.339.4217
www.xulonpress.com

© 2021 by Suzanne S. Bauman

Unless otherwise indicated, Scripture quotations taken from (Version(s) used)

Printed in the United States of America.

Paperback ISBN-13: 978-1-66281-099-2
Ebook ISBN-13: 978-1-66281-100-5

A Smile is powerful.

A Smile can make a shy person feel welcome.

A Smile can lift up
a lonely person's spirit.

A Smile might be
the beginning of
a friendship.

A Smile can change
anger into calmness.

A Smile can heal a
saddened heart.

A Smile says that you are living your life with love.

If you Smile at someone, the chances are very good that your Smile will be returned.

...and suddenly, you will have kinder, warmer hearts.

It's not just people
who Smile...

Dogs Smile.

Dolphins Smile.

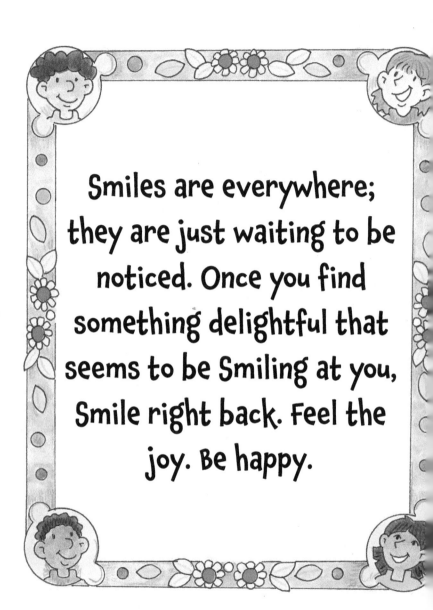

Smiles are everywhere; they are just waiting to be noticed. Once you find something delightful that seems to be Smiling at you, Smile right back. Feel the joy. Be happy.

Now let's have some fun, shall we?

Look around you; use your imagination... how many objects can you see that have the shape of a Smile?

Can you find a Smile in nature? Can you find a Smile in food? Can you find a Smile on a farm? Can you find a Smile in the city? Do animals Smile?

If you look closely, you can see Smiles everywhere you look.

Can you give a Smile away?

Are Smiles contagious?

Look for the Smile
in each of the
following pictures.

As the day turns into gray-green twilight, a swing waits in an empty playground until tomorrow.

A frost-bitten road sign stands like a sentinel against a pewter sky.

Layers of necklaces in all the colors of a desert sunset adorn this pretty miss.

This retired anchor rests in a place of honor after years of preventing ships from drifting.

The wooly Bactrian camel has two plump humps, providing a built-in saddle.

The tough-skinned, slate-gray elephant uses his flexible trunk like an extra arm to feed himself.

A rocking horse has lovingly been set aside until its rider returns for an imaginary adventure.

A cool crescent of watermelon is such a sweet afternoon treat.

A garland, made by braiding evergreen boughs into a rope, is a fragrant holiday decoration.

According to Irish folklore, a horseshoe that is hung with the heels up keeps your luck from flowing out.

Some foods share
their shapes with a
young moon.

Jolly jack-o-lanterns
glowing brightly
welcome ghosts and
goblins on Halloween.
Whooooo!

My own list of things
that have Smiled at me.

My own list of things that have smiled at me.

1. _____
2. _____
3. _____
4. _____
5. _____
6. _____
7. _____
8. _____
9. _____
10. _____

CPSIA information can be obtained
at www.ICGtesting.com
Printed in the USA
LVHW071119290321
682808LV00021B/224